OCEAN

Izzi Howell

D0543120

FACT CAT

Get your paws on this fantastic new mega-series from Wayland!

Join our Fact Cat on a journey of fun learning about every subject under the sun!

Published in paperback in 2017 by Wayland
Copyright © Hodder and Stoughton 2017

Wayland
An imprint of Hachette Children's Group
Part of Hodder & Stoughton
Carmelite House
50 Victoria Embankment
London EC4Y 0DZ

ISBN: 978 0 7502 9467 6
ebook ISBN: 978 0 7502 9466 9
Dewey Number: 333.9'164-dc23
10 9 8 7 6 5 4 3 2 1

Editor: Izzi Howell
Design: Rocket Design (East Anglia) Ltd
Fact Cat illustrations: Shutterstock/Julien Troneur
Other illustrations: Stefan Chabluk
Consultant: Kate Ruttle

Produced for Wayland by
White-Thomson Publishing Ltd
www.wtpub.co.uk
+44 (0) 843 208 7460

An Hachette UK Company
www.hachette.co.uk
www.hachettechildrens.co.uk

Printed and bound in China

Picture and illustration credits:
Dreamstime: Krzysztof Odziomek cover, Zacarias Pereira Da Mata 8, Mikhail Blajenov 10, Elfo724 13 bottom, Rangizzz 14 top left, Pongphan Ruengchai 14 top right; Science Photo Library: Herve Conge/ISM 13, Alexis Rosenfeld 19, Michael Patrick O'Neill 20 top; Shutterstock: Vlad61 title page, Willyam Bradberry 4, Brian Kinney 6 top, Aleksey Stemmer 6 bottom, Matt9122 7, Jeff Schultes 9 left, qingqing 9 right, pierre_j 11, Fiona Ayerst 14 bottom left, Krzysztof Odziomek 14 bottom right, Richard Whitcombe 15, Top Photo Corporation 16, Serge Black 17, Khoroshunova Olga 18, Khoroshunova Olga 21; Stefan Chabluk: 5; Thinkstock: burnsboxco 12, Roi Brooks 20 bottom.

Every effort has been made to clear copyright.
Should there be any inadvertent omission,
please apply to the publisher for rectification.

The author, Izzi Howell, is a writer and editor specialising in children's educational publishing.

The consultant, Kate Ruttle, is a literacy expert and SENCO, and teaches in Suffolk.

FACT CAT FACT

There is a question for you to answer on each spread in this book. You can check your answers on page 24.

CONTENTS

WHAT IS AN OCEAN?

An ocean is a large area of salt water. Animals from this **habitat** can live and breathe underwater.

On the **surface**, the ocean looks calm but underneath it is full of life and movement.

All the salt water on Earth is connected, but we think of it as five different oceans. These are called the Pacific Ocean, the Atlantic Ocean, the Indian Ocean, the Southern Ocean and the Arctic Ocean.

There are three kinds of ocean – tropical, temperate and polar. Each kind of ocean has a different **temperature.**

Arctic Ocean

Atlantic Ocean

Pacific Ocean

Pacific Ocean

Indian Ocean

Southern Ocean

Polar oceans (-2 to 10 °C)
Temperate oceans (10 to 20 °C)
Tropical oceans (20 to 28 °C)

FACT CAT FACT

Salt water is heavier than fresh water. Find out why.

TROPICAL OCEANS

The Indian Ocean, and parts of the Pacific and the Atlantic Oceans, have warm water. These are called tropical oceans. They are home to coral reefs and animals such as sea turtles.

coral

Coral is made up of tiny animals. These animals have hard **exoskeletons** that join together to form the stone-like shapes that make up coral reefs. Find out the name of the world's biggest coral reef.

Clownfish hide from **predators** among sea anemones' **tentacles**.

tentacle

Hammerhead sharks **hunt** for food in tropical oceans. They have sharp teeth to help them catch and eat other ocean animals.

Hammerhead sharks get their name from the shape of their head. The hammer shape means their eyes are far apart. This helps them see a very large area at one time.

FACT CAT FACT

Many types of shark are **endangered** because people catch them to make food from their **fins**.

TEMPERATE AND POLAR OCEANS

Temperate oceans have a mix of warm and cold water because they are between the tropical oceans and the polar oceans. Mackerel, and many other fish that we eat, come from temperate oceans.

Atlantic mackerel live in big groups called schools. The school moves together to find smaller fish and prawns to eat.

The Southern Ocean and the Arctic Ocean are polar oceans. The water there is so cold that it **freezes** sometimes.

Harbour seals can come out of the water to lie on the **ice**. Here, they are safe from killer whales.

Killer whales have fat under their skin that helps them keep warm in the cold polar ocean. Find out what this fat is called.

FACT CAT FACT

Killer whales are not really whales. They are actually a type of dolphin.

WILDLIFE

Many of the animals living in the ocean are fish. Fish have fins and a tail to help them swim. They have **gills** to help them breathe underwater.

This triggerfish uses its tail to push itself forward in the water. Its fins help it to move up and down.

gill

fin

tail

Whales and dolphins have fins and tails, but they are not fish. They come to the surface for air. They breathe through a hole on the top of their head.

Dolphins and whales live in groups called pods. Find out what kind of animal whales and dolphins are.

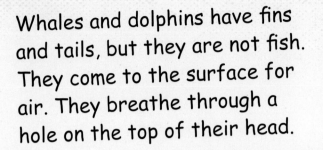

FACT CAT FACT

The blue whale is the biggest animal that has ever lived on Earth. The tongue of a blue whale weighs as much as an elephant.

PLANTS

Seaweed is one of the only plants that grows in the ocean, as most plants can't live in salt water. Seaweed provides food and **shelter** for many ocean animals.

kelp

Kelp is a type of seaweed that covers large areas to form a kelp forest. These forests grow quickly, as one kelp plant can grow up to 25 cm a day.

Some kinds of seaweed have **holdfasts** which help them hold on to rocks. Other types of seaweed move around the ocean, carried by the **currents**.

Seaweed can be green, brown or red. Find out what colour dulse seaweed is.

FACT CAT FACT

Some fish, such as this leafy sea dragon, look like seaweed!

A FOOD CHAIN

Ocean animals and plants get all their food from their habitat. Plants make their own food with the help of sunlight. Ocean animals eat plants or other animals.

Sunlight (makes food for)

Algae (eaten by)

We can use a food chain to see where animals and plants get their food from. Find out the word for animals, such as lemon sharks, that kill other animals for food.

Lemon shark

Parrot fish (eaten by)

Food chains show us how everything is connected in the ocean. Lemon sharks don't eat plants, but plants are still important to them. This is because lemon sharks eat parrot fish who need plants to survive.

This lionfish is keeping its mouth open to catch some of the small fish.

FACT CAT FACT

One parrot fish can make 90 kg of sand every year! Parrot fish eat algae, along with the coral it grows on. This coral is broken into small pieces by the parrot fish's stomach, and these pieces come out as sand.

FOOD FROM THE OCEAN

Many fish that we eat come from the ocean, such as cod and tuna. Every day, fishermen go out on huge boats to catch the fish that we buy from the shops.

Fishmongers are special shops that only sell fish. They have lots of different types of fish to choose from.

Seaweed is very good for you. It has vitamin C, which helps your body stay healthy, and it has calcium that makes your bones strong.

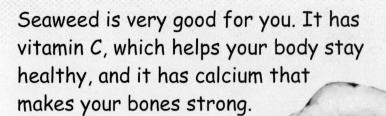

Seaweed is often used in Japanese food. It is wrapped around **raw** fish, vegetables and rice to make a special dish. Find out what this dish is called.

FACT CAT FACT

Lots of tasty foods have seaweed in them, but we can't always see it. We use seaweed in desserts such as ice cream and jelly to give them a firm **texture**.

LEARNING ABOUT THE OCEAN

The ocean is such a big habitat that we still have a lot to learn about it. Scientists have **explored** some of the surface, but we don't know very much about the **deep** ocean.

It's hard for humans to explore the ocean. We can use machines to help us breathe underwater, and wetsuits to help us stay warm.

Submarines help us to travel around the ocean. They can move underwater and **float** on the surface.

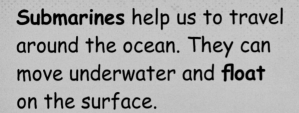

FACT CAT **FACT**

In 1960, two men travelled 10,911 m deep in the ocean in a submarine called the *Trieste*. Find out their names.

Some submarines can spend months underwater! The people in this submarine are studying the **ocean floor**.

PROTECTING THE OCEANS

People often leave rubbish on the seashore and in the ocean. If ocean animals eat the rubbish, they can get sick and die.

It's important to pick up the rubbish that is already in the ocean, and take it back to land.

Recycling or reusing plastic containers means that less rubbish will end up in the ocean, and fewer ocean animals will get hurt.

Many ocean animals are becoming endangered because of the rubbish in the ocean. But if we work together to clean up the oceans, we can help to protect the animals and plants that live there.

Sea turtles are an endangered ocean animal. Find out the name of another endangered ocean animal.

FACT CAT FACT

Sea turtles' eyes sometimes water to help them get rid of extra salt from their bodies.

QUIZ

Try to answer the questions below. Look back through the book to help you. Check your answers on page 24.

1 The Southern Ocean is a polar ocean. True or not true?

a) true

b) not true

2 Clownfish live in polar oceans. True or not true?

a) true

b) not true

3 Fish can breathe underwater. True or not true?

a) true

b) not true

4 Kelp forests grow slowly. True or not true?

a) true

b) not true

5 Seaweed is used to make sushi. True or not true?

a) true

b) not true

6 It is easy for humans to explore the ocean. True or not true?

a) true

b) not true

GLOSSARY

current the natural movement of water

deep when the top and the bottom of something are far apart

endangered something that might become extinct if we don't protect it

exoskeleton a hard outer layer that protects an animal's body

explore to go to a place to find out information about it

fin the triangle-shaped part of a fish that helps it swim

float to stay on the water's surface without sinking

freeze to turn into ice

gills the part of a fish's body that helps it breathe

habitat the place where an animal or plant lives

holdfast the part of seaweed that holds it to a rock

hunt to find and kill animals for food

ice frozen water

ocean floor the land at the bottom of the ocean

predator an animal that kills and eats other animals for food

protect to keep something safe

raw uncooked

shelter a safe place

submarines boats that can travel on and under the water

surface the outside part of something

temperature how hot or cold something is

tentacle a long part of a sea animal's body, similar to an arm

texture how something feels when you touch it

wetsuits clothes that keep you warm underwater

INDEX

ANSWERS

Pages 4–21

Page 4: The salt adds extra weight

Page 6: The Great Barrier Reef

Page 9: Blubber

Page 11: Mammals

Page 13: Red

Page 14: Predator

Page 17: Sushi

Page 19: Jacques Piccard and Don Walsh

Page 21: Many ocean animals, including blue whales, monk seals and bluefin tuna

Quiz answers

1 a) true

2 b) not true, they live in tropical oceans

3 a) true

4 b) not true, they grow very quickly

5 a) true

6 b) not true, it's very difficult